SAND + BONE

SAND + BONE

J.T. KRUL/ANDREA MUTTI

ADAPTIVE COMICS

Written by:
J.T. KRUL

Artwork by:
ANDREA MUTTI

Colors by:
VLADIMIR POPOV

Layout and Lettering by:
CHALLENGING STUDIOS

Cover by:
DENNIS CALERO

Project Managers:
JUSTIN GRAY & JIMMY PALMIOTTI

Design by:
TORBORG DAVERN

Co-published by:
ADAPTIVE STUDIOS

Co-published by PaperFilms & Adaptive Comics. Clearwater, Florida 33759.

Library of Congress Cataloging in Publication Number: 2016962145
ISBN: 978-1-945293-27-6
ebook ISBN: 978-1-945293-26-9
Manufactured in China.
10 9 8 7 6 5 4 3 2 1

Iraq.
THIS IS GREAT. WHERE'S THE DAMN SUPPORT?
SHOOT NOW, CARSON. BITCH LATER.

NO!
ين أجد الصيدلية؟
أضعت طريقي!

فرشتم رعمب كتف
أضعت طريقي!

PERFECT.

CLARKSDALE. THIS IS MY TOWN. WELL, IT WAS.
FEELS DIFFERENT SINCE I GOT BACK.
LIKE I DON'T BELONG. AND THEY'RE NOT MAKING IT EASIER.
SURE, THEY SUPPORT THE TROOPS. IN THEORY.
THEY SMILE.
THEY WEAR THEIR YELLOW RIBBONS.
THEY FLY THEIR FLAGS.
BUT THEY DON'T GIVE A CRAP ABOUT ME. NOT REALLY.
THEY JUST WANT TO FEEL BETTER ABOUT THEMSELVES.
LEM.

NEXT.

SEAN?
HEY, HANNAH. HOW YOU BEEN?

YOU SERIOUS?!
YOU'VE BEEN BACK FOR LIKE WHAT? THREE WEEKS? AND THIS IS HOW YOU COME TO SEE ME? HERE WHILE I AM AT WORK?
I -

NO. LOOK, I'M GLAD YOU'RE BACK AND ALL, BUT YOU DON'T GET TO JUST WALTZ BACK INTO MY LIFE AS EASILY AS YOU WALTZED OUT OF IT.

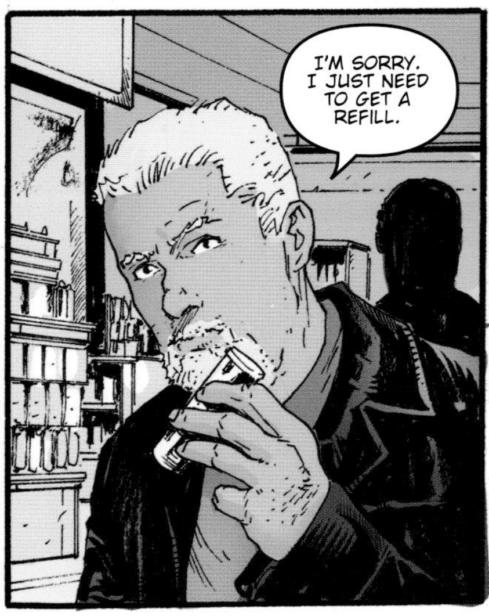
I'M SORRY. I JUST NEED TO GET A REFILL.

I GOT TO CALL IT IN.

BUT, YOU ARE OKAY? RIGHT?

SURE. JUST GOT KNOCKED OUT OF COMMISSION. LEG STILL HURTS, BUT NOTHING A FEW PILLS CAN'T MANAGE. I–

YES? GO AHEAD. UH...HUH. OKAY. THANKS.

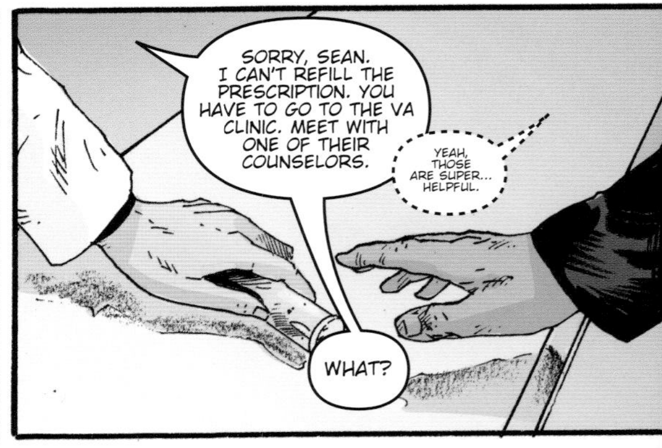
SORRY, SEAN. I CAN'T REFILL THE PRESCRIPTION. YOU HAVE TO GO TO THE VA CLINIC. MEET WITH ONE OF THEIR COUNSELORS.
YEAH, THOSE ARE SUPER... HELPFUL.
WHAT?

NOTHING. THANKS. I'LL SEE YOU AROUND.
YOU GOT THEIR NUMBER? SEAN?
HEY, HANNAH. HOW ABOUT YOU HELP THE NEXT PERSON?

DON'T GET EXCITED, CHARLIE. YOU'LL WASTE YOUR OXYGEN.

Grants
Grants
YEAH, MAN. I HEAR YA.

LIQUOR'S CORNER
MAGAZINE
OH, I'M GOING. I DON'T CARE HOW MUCH THEM TICKETS ARE.
MATCHES.
HUH?

MATCHES.

NAH, NAH, MAN. IT'S COOL. THING DOESN'T EVEN GET JAMMING TIL MIDNIGHT.

Liquors

GRRRR.
GRRR.
YOU GOT A PROBLEM WITH ME, DOG?
FUCK YOU.
ATTA BOY.

CAESAR, GET OVER HERE. YOU JUMP THE FENCE AGAIN?

WHAT UP, MAN? WHATCHA GOT IN THAT BAG?
WHATEVER IT IS, I BET I CAN DO YOU BETTER. GIVE YOU WHAT YOU NEED TO TAKE THE EDGE OFF.
I'M GOOD.

WHAT GIVES, CAESAR?
YO, YOU DO SOMETHING TO MY DOG, MAN? WHY HE ACTING ALL STRANGE?
MAYBE, HE'S JUST SCARED.
PROBABLY SHOULD KEEP HIM ON A SHORTER LEASH.

SCREW YOU, BUDDY. CAESAR IS MY BOY. MINE.
DON'T NEED NOBODY TELLING ME HOW TO TAKE CARE OF HIM. YOU GOT ME?

JUST TRYING TO HELP.

TAP. TAP. TAP. TAP. TAP.
ROLFFF! ROLFFF! ROLFFF!

أين أجد
الصيدلية؟
TWK. TWK. TWK. TWK. TWK. TWK.

أين أجد
الصيدلية؟
TWK. TWK. TWK. TWK. TWK. TWK.
أضعت
طريقي!

TAP. TAP. TAP. TAP.
FF! ROLFF! ROLFF!
TAP. TAP. TAP. TAP. TAP.
ROLFF! ROLFF! ROLFF!
TAP. TAP. TAP. TAP. TAP.
ROLFF! ROLFF! ROLFF!
تعضأ يقيرط!
TWK. TWK. TWK. TWK. TWK. TWK.
دجأ ني ةيلديصلا؟
فرشتم رعمب كتف
تعضأ يقيرط!
THMP. THMP. THMP. THMP. THMP. THMP. THMP. THMP. THMP. THMP. THMP. THMP.

BUNCH OF BS, RIGHT THERE.
I TELL YOU— I'D HAVE THAT BASTARD IN SUCH A CHOKEHOLD LIKE RIGHT QUICK. DUDE BE OUT IN SECONDS. MOST OF THEM UFC FOOLS ARE NOTHING BUT LITTLE BITCHES.
PIZZA
WHEN DID IT START RAINING?
CAESAR! GET THE HELL IN HERE. YER GETTING ALL WET.
DAMMIT, CAESAR, I SAID —
CAESAR
COME O—
AAAAN!

JESUS CHRIST...

CAESAR?!

ROUGH NIGHTS ARE NOTHING NEW TO ME.
HIT IT TOO HARD. WAKE UP IN A POOL OF YOUR OWN PUKE AND PISS.
BUT THIS IS WAY BEYOND THAT.
THIS IS ME OUT OF CONTROL.
HEAD THROBS. BODY ACHES. STOMACH CHURNS.
A BENDER TO END ALL BENDERS...

BAR
JT
OR SO I THOUGHT.
MADE IT THROUGH A COUPLE OF NIGHTS, BUT ENDED UP RIGHT BACK WHERE I STARTED.
WITHOUT MY MEDS, I NEEDED SOMETHING ELSE. SOMETHING TO TAKE IT ALL AWAY.
SOMETHING TO HELP ME FORGET.

A DISTRACTION.

AN ESCAPE.

FROM EVERYTHING.

EVEN FROM MYSELF.

KNK.
KNK.
KNK.
JESUS, YOU LOOK LIKE SHIT.
YOU COME OVER JUST TO SAY THAT?
I CAME OVER TO SEE HOW YOU'RE DOING?
PHARMACISTS MAKE HOUSE CALLS THESE DAYS?
CAN I COME IN?
WHY NOT.
WANT SOMETHING TO DRINK?

I GOT... UM...

WATER.

WHAT HAPPENED AT THE VA? YOU NEVER CAME BACK TO REFILL YOUR PRESCRIPTION.
SO THIS IS A HOUSE CALL.
I'M ASKING AS A... WELL, I DON'T KNOW WHAT WE ARE ANYMORE.
VA WANTED ME TO SIT THROUGH A BUNCH OF THERAPY SESSIONS BEFORE GETTING ANY NEW MEDS. I SAID I'D PASS.
I CAN'T HELP WITH THE MEDS, BUT YOU CAN TALK TO ME.
WORD HAS IT YOU AND ERIC HAMILTON HOOKED UP. EVEN GOT MARRIED.
YEAH. AND DIVORCED.
I HEAR YOU BEEN TROLLING THE DUMPSTERS, SCREWING TRACY ALLEN. STICKING ALL SORTS OF THINGS INTO EACH OTHER.
ANY HOLE IS AS GOOD AS ANOTHER.

GODDAMMIT, SEAN. YOU DON'T GET TO DO THIS. YOU DON'T GET TO BE MAD AT ME.
I MISS YOUR PARENTS, TOO. I WAS RIGHT THERE WHEN THEY DIED. RIGHT AT YOUR SIDE.
I WAS THERE FOR YOU... AND YOU LEFT. YOU RAN OFF AND JOINED THE ARMY. YOU WOULDN'T CALL OR WRITE OR NOTHING. YOU JUST DISAPPEARED. WHAT WAS I SUPPOSED TO DO?
I KNOW.
YOU DIDN'T DO ANYTHING WRONG. I JUST- I COULDN'T BE HERE ANYMORE. COULDN'T BE AROUND THIS TOWN OR ANYBODY. ESPECIALLY YOU.
PEANUTS
BUT THAT'S NOT WHY I DIDN'T COME SEE YOU. LOSING MY PARENTS WAS TOUGH, BUT WHAT I SAW, WHAT I DID OVER IN IRAQ. THAT WAS WORSE.
WAY WORSE.
BUT, YOU SURVIVED, RIGHT?
SOMETIMES, I'M NOT SURE IF I DID OR NOT.
WELL THEN, LET ME HELP YOU FIGURE THAT OUT.

THIS IS NOT A DISCUSSION I'M HAVING AGAIN, ERIC. YOU GOT A PROBLEM WITH IT, TAKE IT UP WITH THE JUDGE.
YOU KEEP THROWING THAT IN MY FACE. GETTING REALLY TIRED OF IT.
REALITY SUCKS, DOESN'T IT.

YOU MAKE TWO DATES TODAY? ME AND ERIC.
IS THAT ANY WAY TO TREAT SOMEONE WHO MANAGED TO GET YOU OUT OF YOUR CAVE?

I SHOULD BE MAD AT YOU. YOU LEFT ME ALL DISTRAUGHT AND I GO AND MAKE THE BIGGEST BAD DECISION OF MY LIFE.
COME ON, THE SOCCER GAME'S ABOUT TO START.
SINCE WHEN ARE YOU A SOCCER FAN?
SINCE MY SON MADE THE TEAM.

WAIT... SON?

LET'S GO, TIGERS!
MOVE THAT BALL!

IS THAT LOOK OF SHOCK ON YOUR FACE FROM SEEING THE SUN FOR THE FIRST TIME IN WEEKS OR FROM LEARNING THAT I'M A MOMMY?
I JUST... I DIDN'T KNOW.
GUESS YOU DIDN'T ASK AROUND ENOUGH ABOUT ME.

YEAH, ERIC IS ONE ROYAL ASSHOLE, BUT I CAN ONLY HATE HIM SO MUCH BECAUSE WE DID MAKE CODY TOGETHER. AND HE'S A GOOD KID.

CODY?!? KICK IT!
A GOOD KID WHO SUCKS AT SOCCER.

SOMETIMES EVEN SHITTY TASTE IN MEN HAS ITS PLUSSES.
UH-UH.
BESIDES, I OCCASIONALLY PICKED A GOOD ONE.

DON'T YOU THINK?

<STOP. STAND DOWN.>
ALLAH!

BOOOOM!

HEEEEY. WHERE YOU BEEN HIDING?
NOT TONIGHT, TRACY.
AW, COME ON. BUY ME A ROUND AND SEE WHERE THE NIGHT TAKES US.
NOPE.
MMMM. GONNA HAVE TO REALLY CONVINCE YOU, AREN'T I?

STOP IT.

WHAT THE FUCK IS YOUR PROBLEM, SON-OF-A-BITCH?
EASY, TRACY.
PRICK.

YOU SAID IT. HE IS A PRICK. TRYING TO SCREW MY WIFE.
EX-WIFE.

SHUT THE HELL UP!

YOU WANNA GO?
BETTER STAY DOWN, OR I'LL FUCKING KILL YOU.

LEAVE ME THE HELL ALONE.

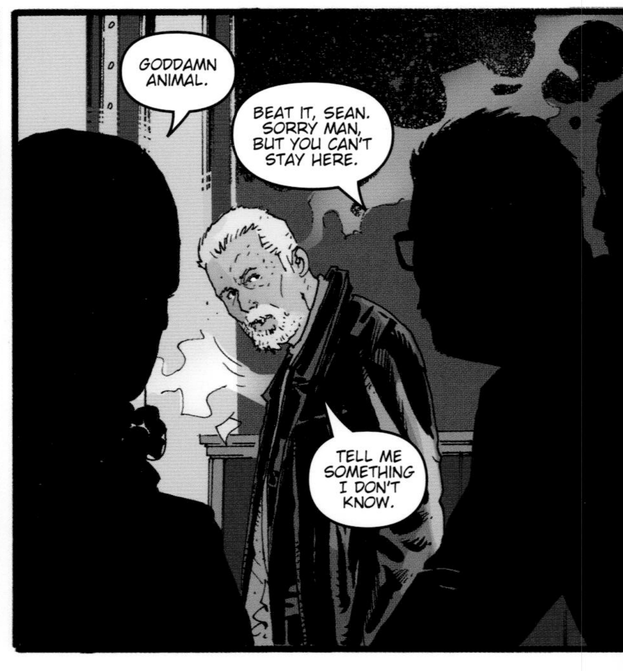
GODDAMN ANIMAL.
BEAT IT, SEAN. SORRY MAN, BUT YOU CAN'T STAY HERE.
TELL ME SOMETHING I DON'T KNOW.

HOW'S IT FEEL YOU BASTARD.

THAT WAS FOR CAESAR.
WH-WHAT ARE YOU TALKING ABOUT?
YOU THINK I'M AN IDIOT?

YOU THINK I DON'T KNOW IT WAS YOU THAT KILLED MY DOG!?

RUN ALL YOU WANT. I'M COMING FOR YOU.

WHERE DID HE GO? I DON'T SEE HIM.
HE'S IN HERE.
WE'RE GOING TO FIND HIM AND WE'RE GOING TO FUCK HIM UP.
YOU HEAR THAT?
I THINK HE'S UP IN THE TREES.
HE AIN'T NO DAMN SQUIRREL.
AIN'T NO WAY YOU'RE GETTING OUT. YOUR ASS IS MINE!

MMMPRH...

NNNN.
KRKKK
COME ON, LOSERS. HE'S JUST ONE GUY.
GET HIM.
NO... NO...NO...

THEY SAY IN DREAMS, RUNNING CAN BE A SYMBOL OF FREEDOM.
BUT NOT IF YOU ARE RUNNING AWAY FROM SOMETHING.
THERE'S NOTHING FREE ABOUT THAT.
IT'S NOT EVEN A DREAM THEN.

IT'S A NIGHTMARE.

I DON'T REMEMBER MUCH OF ANYTHING, EXCEPT...
...EXCEPT RJ'S CRIES.
THEY STICK TO ME... SO DOES THE DIRT AND THE GRIME.
AND SOMETHING TELLS ME THAT I'LL NEVER BE CLEAN. NEVER BE FREE OF IT.
WHATEVER THIS IS- ONE THING'S CLEAR...

I'M LOSING THIS BATTLE.

HANNAH.
pharmacy
SEAN? JESUS. SCARED ME.
SORRY.
WHAT ARE YOU DOING HERE?
I HAD TO GET OUT OF MY APARTMENT, AND I DIDN'T REALLY KNOW WHERE ELSE TO GO.
DID YOU HEAR ABOUT THOSE GUYS THEY FOUND IN THE WOODS?
OF COURSE. IT'S ALL ANYONE'S BEEN TALKING ABOUT ALL WEEK. SOME KIND OF DRUG HIT. HEARD THE POOR BASTARDS GOT MAULED TO DEATH BY DOGS.
I DON'T THINK IT WAS DOGS.
THEN WHAT THEN?
ME.
I THINK.

WHEN I WENT OVERSEAS, THEY WARNED ME THAT THE DESERT COULD PLAY TRICKS ON ME. MESS WITH MY HEAD.
AND, IT DID.

WE WERE AMBUSHED. MY ENTIRE SQUAD WAS KILLED. I TRIED TO HIDE IN A CAVE AND...
...SOME-THING HAPPENED IN THERE.
SOMETHING THAT IS STILL HAPPENING.
I'M SORRY. I SHOULDN'T BE HERE. YOU DON'T NEED TO DEAL WITH ANY OF THIS.
LOOK, SEAN, WE ALL GOT BAGGAGE FROM OUR PAST WEIGHING US DOWN. YOU GOT MORE THAN YOUR SHARE, BUT IT DOESN'T MEAN YOU HAVE TO CARRY IT ALL ALONE.

YOU GOT CODY AND ALL. I SHOULD GO.
I SAID GOODNIGHT TO HIM AN HOUR AGO.
WILL YOU COME INSIDE ALREADY? I JUST HAVE TO PAY THE SITTER AND THEN WE CAN-

ANGIE!!

ANGIE, HONEY? YOU OKAY?
WHERE'S CODY?

THWAP!
HE'S FINE.

WHAT THE HELL IS THE MATTER WITH YOU?!?
NOTHING, BABE. JUST GONNA TAKE CARE OF SOME PERSONAL BUSINESS.

JESUS, ERIC. PLEASE, STOP. CODY IS RIGHT UPSTAIRS.
I KNOW WHERE MY BOY IS.
PLEASE...
AND DON'T GIVE ME THAT MATERNAL INSTINCT CRAP.
IF I HADN'T COME IN WHEN I DID, YOU BE SCREWING HIM ON THE FLOOR... WITH CODY RIGHT UPSTAIRS.
WE WERE SUPPOSED TO BE TOGETHER FOREVER, GODDAMMIT. A FAMILY.
PLEASE... JUST PUT THE GUN DOWN.
BUT, YOU KNOW WHAT? YOU'RE NOTHING BUT A FUCKING WHORE. I DESERVE BETTER.
CODY DESERVES BETTER.
SHOULD BE ME AND HIM. FATHER AND SON. TOGETHER FOREVER.
ONE WAY OR ANOTHER.

ERIC, STOP IT. YOU'RE SCARING HER.
OH, I'M SORRY. WHO THE HELL ARE YOU AGAIN?
OH THAT'S RIGHT. NOBODY.
THIS IS A FAMILY MEETING. DON'T NEED ANY INPUT FROM YOU.
BUT, IF YOU DO WANT TO TALK. I GOT AN ANSWER FOR YOU.
A REAL... LOUD ONE...
NO?
THAT'S WHAT I THOUGHT.

AAAAH!!!
CHMMM
KRREGHKKK!

MOMMY?
C-CODY. WAIT, NO. DON'T COME DOWN HERE.
WHAT'S WRONG?
NOTHING, SWEETIE. IT'S ALL GOOD. STAY UP IN YOUR ROOM. I'LL BE RIGHT THERE.
E-ERIC...?

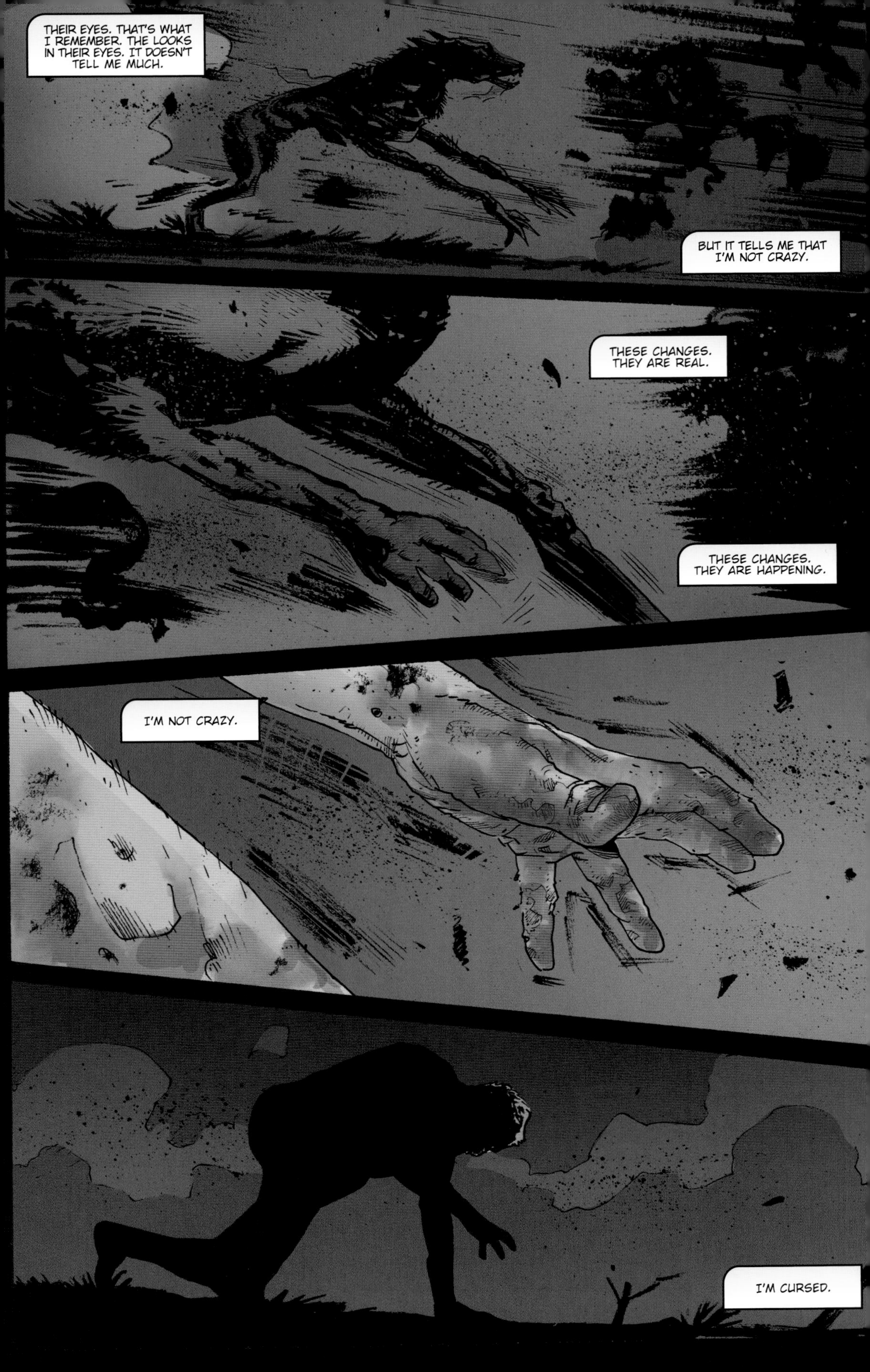
THEIR EYES. THAT'S WHAT I REMEMBER. THE LOOKS IN THEIR EYES. IT DOESN'T TELL ME MUCH.
BUT IT TELLS ME THAT I'M NOT CRAZY.
THESE CHANGES. THEY ARE REAL.
THESE CHANGES. THEY ARE HAPPENING.
I'M NOT CRAZY.
I'M CURSED.

MOM?
MOM! COME ON. WE'RE GOING TO BE LATE.
MOM. WHAT ARE YOU LOOKING AT?
NOTHING, HONEY.
NOTHING.

AS CHILDREN, WE CLOSE OUR EYES WHEN WE ARE SCARED.
THINKING IF WE CAN'T SEE WHAT TERRIFIES US, THEN IT CAN'T SEE US EITHER. OR HARM US.
IT DOESN'T LAST FOREVER.
EVENTUALLY, REALITY FORCES IT'S WAY THROUGH.
AND EVEN IN THE DARKEST OF PLACES-
SKRCH
SKRCH
SKRCH

- THE TRUTH SHINES BRIGHTER THAN ANYTHING.

NIGHT AFTER NIGHT, THE IMAGES RETURN.
ARE THEY VISIONS? MEMORIES? NIGHTMARES?
I CAN'T TELL THE DIFFERENCE ANYMORE.
BUT I DO KNOW ONE THING – I'M LOST.
IN MY WORLD. IN MY MIND. IT'S ALL A MYSTERY.
BUT, THERE'S GOT TO BE ANSWERS. THERE'S GOT TO BE AN EXPLANATION.

AND, I'M GOING TO FIND IT.

J.T. KRUL

is an award-winning, *New York Times* best-selling writer who has worked on such high-profile series as Green Arrow, Captain Atom, Teen Titans, Soulfire, and Superman Beyond. He has published two creator-owned comic books, Jirni and Mindfield, and two novels in his fantasy-adventure series The Lost Spark. He has also worked in animation on various projects, including *Robot Chicken*.

ANDREA MUTTI

has worked for such publishers as DC/Vertigo (The Executor with Jon Evans, and DMZ), Marvel (several Iron Man series), and IDW (G.I. Joe Origins). He also makes comics about everyday life for *Arch+* magazine with Marco Febbrari. He has published two creator-owned series: Rebels with Brian Wood and The Returning with Jason Starr.

VLADIMIR POPOV

is an European based color artist who has worked for publishers such as Boom Studios, Dynamite, Stela, DoubleTake, Soleil, and others on high-profile titles such as Clive Barker's Hellraiser and Next Testament, Robocop, Steed and Mrs. Peel, Adventure Time and Maze Runner.

THE UNITED STATES military has a secret weapon: an individual who wields the superhuman abilities of immense intellect, speed, power, and strength. The cost? His power only lasts forty-five minutes a day. Noah Haller is HYPE, a man who is forced to undergo complete cellular regeneration twenty-three hours each day to retain his capabilities. As Noah works to solve the world's complex problems, he struggles to achieve the emotional balance and understanding that comes naturally to most humans. Scientist Amanda Marr aids him in his journey, but loyalties are tested as a terrorist group threatens the world with a deadly pathogen. *HYPE* is an action-packed thriller from the creative team of Jimmy Palmiotti (*Harley Quinn*, *Painkiller Jane*, *Abbadon*) and Justin Gray (*Forager*, *Wool*, *Jonah Hex*) with visual renderings by Javier Pina (*Birds of Prey*, *Swamp Thing*) and Alessia Nocera (*Abbadon*, *Zenescope Entertainment*).

FROM PROLIFIC WRITERS Jimmy Palmiotti & Justin Gray (*Jonah Hex*, *Power Girl*, *21 Down*) with art by Fabrizio Fiorentino & Alessia Nocera, *Abbadon* tells the tale of a city steeped in sin. The western boomtown of Abbadon is poised for a bright future until it experiences a series of gruesome murders. U.S. Marshal Wes Garrett is called to town to solve them.

A legendary lawman, Garrett is known for having trapped and killed a notorious murderer named "Bloody Bill" who once cut a brutal swath across the country and left scores of mutilated men, women, and children in his wake. Now Garrett's arrival in Abbadon has revealed a secret that Sheriff Colt Dixon has desperately been trying to conceal: the recent murders have all echoed the style of the killer Garrett supposedly stopped years ago. Garrett and Dixon join forces to uncover the killer's identity in a town so full of corruption that everyone is a suspect.

ADAPTIVE
COMICS

PAPERFILMS